Tim's Boat

Written and Illustrated
by Shelley Davidow

Jalmar Press

ISBN 978-1-931061-48-3

Jalmar Press
PO Box 370
Fawnskin, CA 92333
(800) 429-1192
F: (909) 866-2961
www.jalmarpress.com

About the Author and Illustrator: Shelley Davidow is originally from South Africa. Her young adult book, *In the Shadow of Inyangani*, was nominated for the first African Writer's Prize by Macmillan/Picador and BBC World. The author of numerous books, Shelley lives in Florida (USA), where she is a class teacher at the Sarasota Waldorf School.

About the Readers: These early readers are phonetically based and contain stories that young children will find enjoyable and entertaining. Each story has a beginning, middle and an ending. The stories are gently humorous while honoring nature, animals and the environment.

The six books use simple words that the early reader will easily grasp. They have been carefully chosen by a reading specialist to help students advance from the short vowels, to the silent "e", to the vowel combinations. At the back of this book is a list of sight words that should be reviewed with the child before reading the book.

About our Reading Specialist: Mary Spotts has been a remedial reading teacher for over ten years, taking countless classes and seminars to keep current in the field she loves. Her deep under-standing that struggling readers need good stories — particularly if the books are phonetically based — has been an inspiration in the creation of these books. Mary has been a constant guide, ensuring that the books address specific phonetic principles while retaining a gently humorous story line.

Mary's desire to have available meaningful children's stories with decodable words and Shelley's creative talents and love of literature have been the incentive and encouragement to bring these books to production.

For Tim

m had a boat.

m went with his boat to the pond at the tree.

t the pond he dug a deep moat for his boat.

ιe boat did not float, for the boat had a hole.

"Let me fix this," said Tim, and he ran home.
A green toad saw Tim run.

Tim's B

Tim took his boat and went into the shed.
He fixed the hole in the boat.
Then he came out of the shed.

"Let me see if the boat floats," he said.
He ran to the pond.

Tim's B

Tim set the boat into the moat.
His feet got wet in the pond.
"Look! My boat floats."
The green toad saw Tim.
Tim saw the toad.

The boat went from the moat into the pond.
Then the boat went to the green toad.

Tim's Bo

Tim saw the green toad get onto the boat.
"Go toad," said Tim. "Go for a ride."

The green toad went for a
ride on the boat in the pond.
The toad went from the pond to the moat.
Rain came, but Tim did not go home.

Tim ran to the moat.

"Do you like this boat, toad?

You can sail on the boat if you like, toad.

This is a Green Toad Boat."

But then Tim and the toad saw a snake.

The snake saw the boat and the toad.

The snake swam to the boat in the rain.

Tim saw the rain soak the boat.

Tim's B

The green toad got off the boat.

The snake slid onto the boat.

The toad swam to the pond.

The snake sat on the boat.

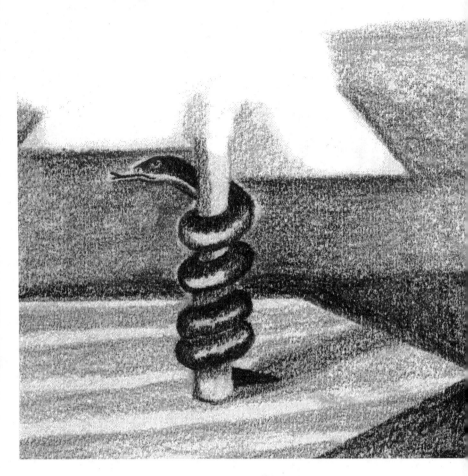

"Go for a ride, snake," said Tim.

"This is a Toad Boat and a Snake Boat.

Can you sail the boat, snake?"

Tim's Bo

The snake went for a ride on the boat.

A bee saw the snake on the boat.

The bee went to sit on the boat.

The snake saw the bee,

and the snake slid into the deep pond.

Tim got his boat and said,"this is a boat for three
A green toad, a snake and a bee went for a ric
and a sail on my boat in the rain. I like my boa
It is a good boat. It floats and sails."
Then Tim went home with wet feet and
went to sleep.

14

Short Vowel Sounds

a	e	i	o	u
can	set	if	off	dug
	shed	Tim	pond	run
	let	fix (ed)		

Silent "e"	ee	oa	Sight Words
ride	bee	toad	me
	see	boat	took
	tree	moat	look
	three	soak	from
	feet	floats	good
	green		sails
	deep		out
	sleep		

9 781931 061483